Banderillas, piperrada, empanadas, gambas a la plancha, tortilla de patatas, albóndigas and many more authentic recipes for deliciously, delectable Spanish appetizers and snacks.

Tapas!

Editors **Margriet van Aalten,
Jessica Verbruggen, Marianna Wesselink**
Editorial Board **Anda Schippers,
Marjan Terpstra**
Art Direction/design **Kirsti Alink**
Photography **Food4Eyes.com,
Mark van Stokkom**
Food **Francis van Arkel, Rob Beernink,
Thea Spierings**
Styling **Heidi Heymans-Timmermans,
Moniek Visser, Lize Boer**
Editor **Pieter Harts**

© Visconti, 2008
1st printing 2008

© English edition: Miller Books
email: info@miller-books.com
www.miller-books.com

978 90 8724 052 3

"Si no puedes improvisar, no puedes cocinar If you can't improvise, you can't cook. Tapas! Over eighty recipes offering infinite possibilities.

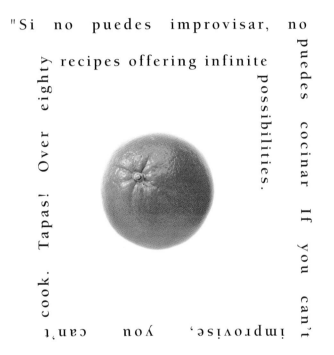

Foreword

When are Spaniards truly in their element? When they're enjoying great appetizers with a glass of sherry while happily chatting with friends. However, this isn't about any old appetizer made from some ordinary recipe or some type of mini-starter. No, this is about tapas: tasty, individual dishes that are served in countless variations throughout Spain's many tapas bars.

Tapas are as important a part of the day in Spanish life as breakfast, lunch, siesta and dinner; in fact, possibly more so. However small or simple the tapas may be, they represent a certain attitude: a relaxed lifestyle, where time is made to enjoy tasty food in relaxed company. This style seems to have worldwide appeal: from London to New York tapas bars are constantly being built. Wherever you go, tapas bars are springing up everywhere.

This cookery book, with its many traditional but also astonishingly contemporary tapas dishes, is intended to meet the growing demand in creating a Spanish-style evening. It can be as simple as a couple of slices of chorizo and olives on a cocktail, or maybe something a little more complicated, such as prawns with romesco sauce. It just depends what you want!

Contents

The taste of

TAPAS

Walk into a tapas bar in any given Spanish city on a summer's evening at around eight o'clock and you will be overwhelmed by the hustle and bustle, the sherry and the smell of the fresh tortillas, pollo al ajillo and fried calamaras. All of these are universally known tapas, chalked up on the blackboard by every dueño. People are at the bar, with their noses pressed up against the glass displays, in which the house specialities are prominently displayed. Elsewhere on the premises, incoming guests are welcomed loudly, while tapas are consumed one after the other in an almost cursory fashion, washed down with a traditional sherry, a good glass of wine or a cerveza. During heated discussions, differences of opinions are explored, embraces exchanged and philosophical subjects touched upon. Under foot, the shells crunch on the ground. Meanwhile, the cook does their best to keep up with the tempo of the diners as the waiters rack their brains to remember who ate what. No matter where you are around eight o'clock, Spain will be alive.

Central to this is the tapa. Whether it is glamorous or simple, this traditional appetizer is always very varied as well as tasty, and is consumed at least once a day by the average Spaniard.

The salt of the tapa encourages the desire for a drink

There are various stories about the origins of tapa. This small snack was supposedly created for the corpulent King Alfonso X of Castilia, who, for health reasons, considered it more sensible to eat smaller portions. That the Arabs, who settled in Spain around 711, brought the tapas culture with them sounds slightly more plausible. For the Arabs, it is a gesture of hospitality to present your guest with some snacks. However, the veteran Spanish consumer of tapas will tell you that the tradition originates from Andalusia during the nineteenth century, where it is inextricably linked with the traditional drink from this region: sherry. To keep the sherry free of flies for their guests, the Andalusian dueños covered the full glasses with a piece of jamón Serrano, a practice welcomed by everyone. The guests received a free snack (the word tapa comes from tapar, to cover), café owners across the country soon noticed that the salt of the tapa encouraged the desire for a drink, and a profitable tradition was born.

The tapa was originally very simple: a piece of ham, a slice of chorizo. Over the centuries, many variations have been created. Moreover, the art of tapas was not restricted to Southern Andalusia. It extended into the extremely well-versed culinary areas of Galicia and the Basque Country and then eventually the rest of Spain. Consequently, you can now order in any given tapas bar a tortilla, empanada or gambas a la plancha without a problem. They are the most well-known tapas, the recipes of which are etched in stone in the memory of every cook.

The tapa is deeply interwoven with the social life and the culture of Spain. Food is important to the Spanish. They live from meal to meal. Starting with a light breakfast around eight o'clock in the morning, life is put on hold at around one o'clock for the first tapas, followed by a full lunch. At the beginning of the evening, the appetite is stimulated once more with tapas, after which the day is ended with a late dinner. The tapa fits in with the Spanish character and way of life. Without relying on stereotypes, the tapa is emblematic of hospitality, friendly get-togethers, joy, taste and style. Tapas is called an art; it is almost a religious act, where improvisation is permissible. This is not unusual to the Spanish. There are no rules and regulations, as these are preferably ignored. The tapa is also part of the Spanish

life outside of the home. Whereas North Europeans are used to inviting friends and acquaintances into their homes and much of their social lives take place inside, most Spaniards frequently meet in public places. Even business meetings are in public. Where better can you discuss a business issue than in a bar?

A good tapas bar is recognisable by the following features, with even the name being an indication. A bodegón is more of a drinking establishment where there is only a limited tapas menu on offer. A mesón is a rustic place, where there is a tapas bar as well as restaurant. Tasca on the other hand designates a real tapas bar. If there are Iberian pork hams and home-made salamis hanging from the ceiling, then you can be reassured that the quality of food is well above average. And if the dueños' specialities are written in white paint on the windows or on a blackboard, then you can be sure of its authenticity.

The only fundamental change with regards to tapas is that they are no longer free. For the rest, the tapa and its processes have undergone little in the way of tampering. The constant refinement of nouvelle cuisine has not oppressed the tapa. Moreover, the enormous rise of fast-food chains over the past

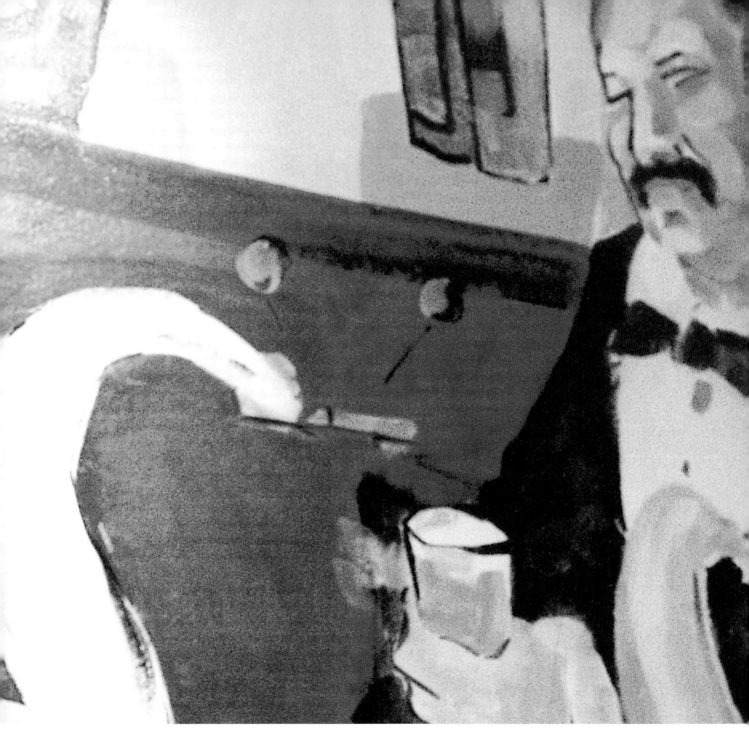

twenty years has not shifted the tapa from its number one spot as a quick snack. Preferable to grabbing a plastic hamburger at their desk for lunch, the Spanish will leave their duties and duck quickly into a tapas bar to hear the latest gossip or to see a friend before going home to have a full family lunch in the privacy of their home. Is the tapa an endangered phenomenon?

It would appear to be quite the contrary. In fact, new, surprising, tasty and unusual tapas are constantly being created. Not only as the various Spanish regions jumped on the tapas bandwagon and introduced more of their own creations, but also as the tapa was enjoyed worldwide, new tastes were developed many thousands of kilometres from the tapa-epicentre of Andalusia.

Spanish culinary tradition

As with every country in the world, Spain is not closed off from the rest of world and its influences. In particular, the Roman occupation and later the Arabs (from 8th until 15th century) had a deep impact on the country. The contribution from the Romans was in fact quite modest, with their introduction of the olive-tree as well as conservation methods of the olives. The Arabs left greater influences, especially in Andalusia where these are particularly strong. They brought

many foodstuffs with them: honey, almonds, hazelnuts, citrus fruits and sugar cane and spices such as caraway, cinnamon, black pepper, saffron and nutmeg. These are of course all the ingredients, which are to be found in the kitchens of every chef today. Moreover, it was due to the Moorish invention of a clever irrigation system in the region of Valencia that rice as an ingredient – and thus the invention of paella as a dish – was introduced to Spanish cooking. And then there was of course Columbus who brought back tomatoes, peppers, potatoes, corn, beans, avocados and chocolate from his journeys to South America.

Add this all to the native foodstuffs and there is quite a simple, varied, refined, rich and exciting cuisine, which is amongst other things reflected in these absolutely delicious tapas.

Is the tapa under threat? On the contrary!

There is a saying: 'If you can't improvise, you can't cook.' With the tapa, there are endless possibilities. The only prerequisite is that the different tastes must complement each other. Apart from that, practically everything is possible. And that is precisely why the tapa has been able to retain such an informal nature. Tapas don't need to be small or to be restricted to certain ingredients. In fact, there are as many tapas as there are cooks. However, that doesn't mean that the tapas can't be classified into categories. They can be grouped by cooking methods: tapas in sauces; pastry tapas; cold tapas; warm tapas; deep-fried tapas; grilled tapas; marinated tapas. But the manner of presentation is also important. There are tostadas (nearly anything on a piece of bread is immediately classifiable

as a tostada), banderillas (marinated fish, olives, vegetables etc on a cocktail stick) and tapas which are served in shells. It is particularly important to mention the varying sizes of the portions. If you order tapa, tapita or montados, then you will get served the original quantity. Ask for a ración, and then you can expect a portion twice the size of a tapa portion. If you're extremely hungry then go for the porción as this resembles a complete meal.

Every city or region has its own specialities and customs in the use of tapas. The coastal regions are famous for their tapas with fish and shellfish, whereas in the Spanish countryside you can count on tapas with beef, pork, vegetables and nuts.

In the region from where tapa originates, you will find the best tapas bars as a rule. Seville is world famous for its tapas. Nowhere else in Spain is tapas such a constant part of daily life as in this city. The real classics such as albóndigas, riñones al jerez and of course the extremely well-known jamón serrano come from here. This particular tapa comes from the pata negra (a type of pig with black legs) and is traditionally served with a cold glass of fino (dry sherry). When ordering in Seville, you still regularly will receive a dish of almendras fritas on the house: a very popular tapa in Seville.

Apart from Seville, Madrid is also renowned for its tapas. The tapa culture forms an indispensable part

of the nightlife; it is known as la movida (translates as: the movement). After work, the people of Madrid first have an aperitivo in a tapas bar and then go from café to café in search of sociability,

casually munching on new snacks along the way. In the many cervecerías with which Madrid is rich, the bocadillos and the montaditos form a true cult. These warm pieces of bread are available with meat or fish; the cold alternatives – such as tuna in oil with tomato and bread – are very popular as fast-food.

In less urban areas such as Galicia and Extremadura, the rural kitchen is dominated by plenty of beef, mutton, lamb and goat. With its wild climate and an ensuing need for hearty fare, there has never been a real tapas culture here. Here, the tapas are coarser and simpler and are still handed out free. Well-known snacks are the

empanadas from Galicia and not to be forgotten the chorizo from Extremedura. This spicy seasoned salami with garlic and paprika is available in many variations: fresh, dry or smoked, as a pâté on bread or eaten just as it is.

A more modern, fusion orientated tapas cooking style can be found in Barcelona. All the same, patatas bravas will still be found on the menu in this metropolis. These patatas are frequently served with the famous alioli, a garlic and olive oil sauce. In Catalonia, tapas are generally served at a table as a starter rather than standing at a bar. As an accompaniment, a cold glass of cava is usually served; this sparkling wine originates from the region around Barcelona, and is made according to the traditional champagne method.

In Northern Spain, the tapas have more the character of an amuse-bouche. In particular, the Basque Country leads the way with refined tapas, also known as pinchos. The word pinchos comes from the verb pinchar, which means to prick or stab. Pieces of white bread are

Making Tapas Yourself

And now it's time to try some tapas ourselves. You can have tapas as a snack with drinks, as a side-dish during the meal or as a main meal. We may not be doing justice to the Spanish use of the tapa where it is served as an entrée to a more extensive meal. But then what is more delicious than a table full with a staggering array of tapas by which you can intensively sample the taste of Spain? ¡Buen provecho!

carefully stacked with all sorts of ingredients – frequently vegetables, shellfish and hardboiled egg – and are then held together with a cocktail stick. These impressive tower-like constructions are eaten without a plate using your fingers.

In regions such as La Mancha and Asturia, cheeses such as manchego and cabrales are favourite tapas. In the old days, the shepherds of La Mancha happily used manchego (made from sheep milk) as provisions, because of its shelf life. This cheese is preferably eaten on its own, and if absolutely necessary only accompanied by a glass of red wine or sherry; this in contrast to the blue cheese cabrales, which in Asturia is washed down with the well-known sidra (cider) from this region in Barcelona.

Tapas con pan

Tapas with bread

Makes 15 servings ★ 500g flour ★ 7g dried yeast ★ 1 teaspoon salt ★ 1 teaspoon sugar ★ 2 tablespoon

Coca con sobrasada
Griddle Cake with Sausage

Coca is a Balearic griddlecake which is often served with vegetables, meat or fish, but also frequently as a sweet dish. In Mallorca, it is frequently eaten with the famous national sausage Sobrasada. This is a mild salami, seasoned with garlic and pepper. Sobrasada is also commonly eaten as a tapa, with just a little bit of bread.

1 Mix the flour, yeast, salt and sugar.
2 Then add in the oil, wine and water, and knead into a smooth paste.
3 Roll this paste into a griddle cake and place it onto a baking tray.
4 Cover with olive oil and then put the sausage slices on top.
5 Allow the griddle cake to rise for 15-20 minutes and then bake the cake in an oven at 200°C for 25-30 minutes until done.

Pan con tomate

Bread with tomato

1 Cut the bread into slices and then toast them under the grill until they are crispy.
2 Rub the slices of bread with fresh garlic, tomato and salt, and then sprinkle them with olive oil.

Catalonians are raised on pan con tomate. They make it with Catalonian farmer's bread: firm, oval and absolutely delicious. Bread with tomato is eaten with every meal or else plain with pieces of anchovies, cheese or Serrano ham.

white farmer's bread ★ Garlic, peeled ★ Tomato, cubed ★ Salt ★ Olive oil

Pan con anchoas

Bread with anchovies

1 Bake the sliced bread with some olive oil on a pre-warmed baking tray at 200ºC.
2 On each piece of bread, put some anchovies, chopped garlic, tomato, parsley and a dash of lemon juice.

1 tomato, chopped int ★ Lemon juice ★ 1 clove of garlic, peeled ★ 4 tins of anchovies ★ or baguette

Pan con alioli

Bread with garlic mayonnaise

Alioli is eaten throughout Catalonia with both meat and fish dishes. These days you'll find alioli served with bread more and more frequently on menus in tapas bars.

1 Peel the garlic cloves and either grind them in a mortar or crush them in a garlic press.
2 Add the lemon juice, egg yolks and a little bit of fresh pepper, and mix this in with the garlic.
3 Using a whisk add a little bit of oil slowly until the mayonnaise thickens.
4 Add salt to taste.
5 Serve with pieces of baguette.

Tip: By first cooking the garlic in the oven the sauce loses its pungent fresh garlic taste, giving it a sweeter flavour. This method also ensures that you won't smell of garlic the following day. Make the sauce as described above but before you start, wrap the unpeeled garlic in aluminium foil and place it in a warm oven (180°C) for 20 minutes. The garlic cloves will soften, both in taste and texture.

Tostada con chorizo
Toast with sausage

1 Mix the flour, yeast, sugar and water and knead into a supple dough.
2 Place the mix into a baking dish and leave to rise for 30-45 minutes.
3 Bake it in an oven at 200°C for approximately 25 minutes until done.
4 Leave the bread to cool down once it has been take out of the oven.
5 In the meantime, fry the chopped garlic together with the shallots and the mushrooms in olive oil for 2-3 minutes. Season with pepper, salt and vinegar.
6 Cut the bread into slices and spread the olive oil, garlic, pepper and salt on top.
7 Bake the slices in the oven until brown at 200°C for approximately 10 minutes.
8 Cover the bread with the sausage and serve with dressing.

Pan de queso de cabra

Goat's cheese bread

Makes 15 servings ★ 500g baking flour ★ 1 teaspoon of salt ★ 2 tablespoon of coarsely, ground black pepper ★ 1 tablespoon of sugar ★ 1 egg ★ 60g soft butter ★ 150g soft goat's cheese, crumbled ★ 250 g spinach leaves, chopped ★ 125ml milk (goat or cow's milk) ★ 200ml water

1 Mix the baking flour, salt, pepper and sugar in a bowl.
2 Stir the butter and egg into the mix.
3 Then mix in the goat's cheese, spinach leaves, milk and water.
4 Knead into a smooth soft dough.
5 Place the dough in a bread tin and bake in the oven at 200°C for 30-35 minutes.
6 Slice the bread and then again cut into strips.
7 Serve the bread as is or place the strips under the grill again before serving.

cloves of garlic ★ 250 ml dry white wine ★ 2 tablespoon of olive oil ★ 1-2 smoked fillets of trout ★

12 pieces baguette ★ Black pepper ★ 2 tablespoons of chives, chopped

4 whole

2 red pimientos (grilled pepper, see recipe on page 47), in pieces ★

Makes 12 servings ★

Tostada con trucha

Trout on toast

Walk into any bar in the Basque Country and you will find tapas with fried bread everywhere. These tostadas (literally: toast), frequently served with anchovies, tuna or trout, are eaten just like that, without even a plate. They are extremely tasty and are very easy to make. Pinchos are also bread tapas: however several ingredients are stacked on top of each other instead.

1 Cook the garlic with the wine until the wine is almost completely evaporated.
2 Mash the garlic and olive oil together into a puree. Season with pepper.
3 Break up the trout fillets into large pieces.
4 Toast the bread in the oven at 220°C for 6-8 minutes.
5 Spread the garlic paste on the bread.
6 Put pieces of fish and pimientos on top; sprinkle with chives and pepper.

Tip: As an alternative you can replace the fish with goat's cheese.

Per cocktail stick ★ 1 small slice of baguette ★ 1 slice of Serrano ham ★ 1 slice of smoked salmon ★ 2 slices of hardboiled egg ★ 1 prawn

Pinchos de huevo y salmón

Egg and salmon on a cocktail stick

1 Toast the baguette under the grill, with some olive oil and crushed garlic as required.
2 Line up the ingredients in the following order: Serrano ham, smoked salmon, prawn, egg slices.
3 Garnish with mayonnaise.
4 Put a cocktail stick through the ingredients.

cocktail stick ★ 1 ★ peeled and cooked ★ Mayonnaise ★ Olive oil (for seasoning) ★ Garlic, crushed (for seasoning) ★ 1

of egg ★ 1 tin of anchovies, (anchovies sliced down the middle) ★ 5 prawns, cooked and peeled ★ Mayonnaise ★ Parsley, chopped ★ Olive oil (for

Pinchos de gambas y anchoas

Prawn and anchovy on a cocktail stick

1 Toast the baguette under the grill, with a little bit of olive oil and crushed garlic.
2 Place the egg, prawns and anchovies on top.
3 Garnish with mayonnaise and parsley.
4 Thread all the ingredients together on a cocktail stick.

Vamos de pinchos! is Spanish expression for 'Come on, let's eat some tapas!'

Per cocktail stick ★ 1 piece of baguette ★ 2 slices ★ seasoning) ★ Garlic, crushed (for seasoning) ★ 1 cocktail stick

Per cocktail stick ★ 1 slice of baguette ★ 1 slice of Serrano ham ★ 1 slice of tomato ★ 1 tinned or fresh aspa-

Pinchos de espárragos y tomate

Asparagus and tomato on a cocktail stick

ragus cut in pieces ★ 1 slice of hardboiled egg ★ Mayonnaise ★ Parsley, chopped. ★ Olive oil (for seasoning) ★ Garlic, crushed (for seasoning) ★ 1 cocktail stick

Tip: Not everyone may like the combination of cabrales and anchovy. If you're in any doubt, you can always try some goat's cheese or a mild blue cheese. If you don't like fish, you can replace the anchovies with pimientos (roasted pepper, see the recipe elsewhere in the book). As an alternative you can also serve the pinchos de cabrales y jamón serrano warm. Put the prepared bread and toppings under the grill for approximately 2 minutes. You don't need to use the cocktail stick for these.

1 Toast the baguette under the grill, with a little olive oil and crushed garlic.
2 Put the Serrano ham, tomato, asparagus, and egg on top.
3 Garnish with mayonnaise and parsley.
4 Thread all the ingredients together on a cocktail stick.

★ Garlic, crushed (for seasoning) ★ 1 cocktail stick

Pinchos de cabrales y jamón serrano

Cabrales and Serrano ham on a cocktail stick

Per cocktail stick ★ 1 slice of baguette ★ 1 slice of Serrano ham ★ 1 slice of cabrales (Spanish cheese) ★ 1 tin of anchovies, anchovies sliced down the middle ★ Olive oil (for seasoning)

1 Toast the baguette under the grill, with a little olive oil and crushed garlic.
2 Put the Serrano ham, cabrales and anchovy fillet on top.
3 Thread all the ingredients together on a cocktail stick.

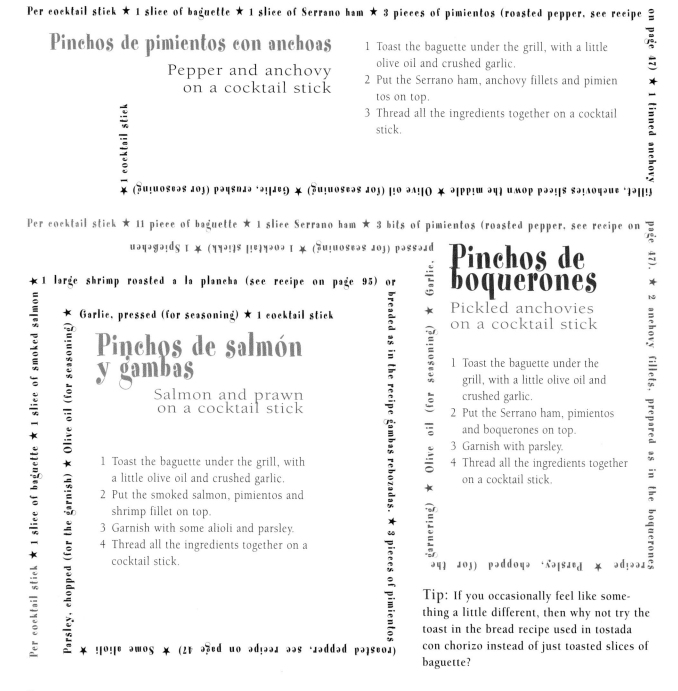

Pinchos de pimientos con anchoas
Pepper and anchovy on a cocktail stick

1 Toast the baguette under the grill, with a little olive oil and crushed garlic.
2 Put the Serrano ham, anchovy fillets and pimientos on top.
3 Thread all the ingredients together on a cocktail stick.

Per cocktail stick ★ 11 piece of baguette ★ 1 slice Serrano ham ★ 3 bits of pimientos (roasted pepper, see recipe on page 47). ★ 1 large shrimp roasted a la plancha (see recipe on page 95) or breaded as in the recipe gambas rebozadas. ★ 3 pieces of pimientos (roasted pepper, see recipe on page 47) ★ Garlic, pressed (for seasoning) ★ 1 cocktail stick ★ 1 Spiesbchen

Per cocktail stick ★ 1 slice of baguette ★ 1 slice of smoked salmon ★ Olive oil (for seasoning) ★ Parsley, chopped (for the garnish) ★ Some alioli

Pinchos de salmón y gambas
Salmon and prawn on a cocktail stick

1 Toast the baguette under the grill, with a little olive oil and crushed garlic.
2 Put the smoked salmon, pimientos and shrimp fillet on top.
3 Garnish with some alioli and parsley.
4 Thread all the ingredients together on a cocktail stick.

Pinchos de boquerones
Pickled anchovies on a cocktail stick

1 Toast the baguette under the grill, with a little olive oil and crushed garlic.
2 Put the Serrano ham, pimientos and boquerones on top.
3 Garnish with parsley.
4 Thread all the ingredients together on a cocktail stick.

page 47). ★ 2 anchovy fillets, prepared as in the boquerones recipe ★ Parsley, chopped (for the garnering) ★ Olive oil (for seasoning) ★ Garlic,

Tip: If you occasionally feel like something a little different, then why not try the toast in the bread recipe used in tostada con chorizo instead of just toasted slices of baguette?

Tapas con verduras

Tapas with vegetables

Pimientos

Slivers of red pepper cooked in the oven

chopped ★ 1 tablespoon of lemon juice or wine vinegar ★ Freshly ground pepper and salt

Makes 8 servings ★ 4 red peppers ★ 100ml olive oil ★ 1 clove of garlic,

1 Heat the oven to 180°C.
2 Place the red peppers in an oven dish and put them in the oven for 20 minutes. Turn them and then let them cook for another 20 minutes.
3 Take them out of the oven, cover them with a cloth or aluminium foil and allow them to cool down.
4 Take the peppers out of the dish; keep the juices for the dressing.
5 Peel the peppers and cut them into strips.
6 The pimientos are now ready for further use.

In Spain, oven-cooked pimientos are eaten as a side dish with pork cutlets or tuna but also frequently served as tapa. The peppers are softened and sweetened in the oven. This tapa taste best when served at room temperature.

Preparation of the dressing

1 Put the juice from the peppers in a bowl.
2 Add garlic and wine vinegar or lemon juice.
3 Using a whisk mix and add in olive oil to the dressing until the desired consistency has been achieved.
4 Season with salt and freshly ground pepper.
5 Pour the sauce over the peppers.

Berenjenas fritas Deep-fried aubergines

Makes 12 servings ★ 1 aubergine ★ Salt and pepper ★ Lemon juice ★ Flour ★ Milk ★ Oil for frying

1 Peel the aubergine and cut it into thin slices.
2 Sprinkle the slices on each side with salt and lemon juice and put them aside on a plate, covered with another plate on top. Leave the aubergine for about an hour so that the moisture is drawn out of the aubergine.
3 Dry the aubergine slices with cooking paper.
4 Mix the sifted flour with sufficient milk to make a thick batter.
5 Season the batter with salt and pepper.
6 Heat the oil in a pan. You can use either a high-sided pan or a deep-fat fryer; however ensure that the pan has at least 0.5cm of oil in it.
7 Fry the aubergine slices on each side until they are brown.
8 Serve immediately.

Alcachofa adobada

Marinated artichoke hearts

1 Take the artichokes out of the tin and drain well.
  Slice them once through the middle.
2 Combine the olive oil, basil and garlic.
3 Add the artichokes and leave to marinade for 1 hour.
4 Serve in a dish with thick chunks of bread.

halved ★ 2 red peppers, halved, deseed, cut into 12 pieces ★ 2 or 3 tablespoons of olive oil ★ 12 small wooden cocktail sticks ★ 1 tablespoon of parsley, chopped ★ Sea salt

Makes 12 servings ★ 24 small new potatoes, unpeeled ★ 12 garlic cloves peeled ★ 6 shallots, peeled and

Patatas con ajo
Potatoes with garlic

1 Cook the potatoes.
2 Fry the halved shallots with the garlic cloves for 2-3 minutes until they just before they soften.
3 Thread 12 small skewers with garlic, potato, pepper and shallot.
4 Marinate the skewers in 2-3 tablespoons of olive oil.
5 Grill the skewers over an open fire or in a hot pan.
6 Sprinkle with chopped parsley and salt.

Champiñones rellenos

Stuffed mushrooms

the caps whole ★ 2 onions chopped into small pieces ★ 3 garlic cloves, crushed ★ 250g chorizo, cut into pieces and

1 Fry the onion and mushroom stalks in olive oil until all the moisture has disappeared.
2 Add the chorizo and garlic and leave to cook at a low temperature for approximately 6 minutes until well-done.
3 Season with salt and pepper.
4 Fill the caps with the chorizo mix and then place them in an oven dish.
5 Bake them for 10 minutes in a pre-heated oven at 180°C.
6 Garnish the caps with pimientos.

without skin ★ 1 tablespoon of pimientos (roasted pepper, see recipe on page 47), in small pieces. ★ Pepper and salt ★ Olive oil

Makes 12 servings ★ 2 large mushrooms – chop the stalks into small pieces and keep

Ensalada de pimientos y tomate

Pepper and tomato salad

Makes 4 servings ★ 3 tablespoon of pimientos (roasted pepper, see recipe on page 47), in strips ★ 1 small onion, in thin rings ★ 4 mid-sized tomatoes cut into eighths ★ Salt and freshly ground pepper ★ 3 tablespoons of olive oil ★ 2 tablespoons of red wine vinegar ★ 1 teaspoon of sugar ★ 3 anchovy fillets, washed and chopped finely ★ 1 tablespoon of parsley, finely chopped ★ 12 or more olives

1 Place the strips of pimientos in layers in a shallow dish with a flat base.
2 Place the onion rings on top of the pimientos.
3 Place the chopped tomatoes on top of the onions and sprinkle salt and pepper over them.
4 Mix the oil, vinegar, sugar, salt, pepper and anchovies in a small bowl.
5 Pour this mixture over the vegetables. Sprinkle the salad with parsley and then garnish with olives.
6 Leave the salad in the refrigerator for a couple of hours before serving.

Makes 12 servings ★ 400g potatoes ★ 1 tin of tuna ★ 1 small onion, chopped ★ 1 clove of garlic, chopped ★ 1 tablespoon of parsley, chopped ★ 1 teaspoon of red wine vinegar ★ 1 teaspoon of capers ★ 1 tablespoon of mayonnaise ★ Black olives and pimientos to garnish ★ Pepper and salt ★ 2 hardboiled eggs, chopped ★ pimientos (roasted pepper, see recipe on page 47) ★ 2 tablespoon of gherkins, cut (or cocktail onions) ★ 2 tablespoons of peas ★ 1 tablespoon of cubed

Ensalada Rusa Russian salad

In Spain, salads made with mayonnaise are often eaten as a tapa. The salads are often eaten as they are, however they are also regularly used as filling for empanadas or simply spread onto a tostada.

1 Boil the potatoes for 20 minutes until they are done.
2 Leave them to cool down and then cut them into cubes.
3 Mix the tuna, onion, garlic, parsley, vinegar, capers, gherkins, peas, pimientos and eggs in a dish.
4 Add the potatoes and stir well.
5 Season with pepper, salt and mayonnaise according to taste.
6 Garnish with olives and pimientos.
7 Serve at room temperature.

Higos con queso de cabra y almendras

Figs with goat's cheese and almonds

The combination of a strong goat's cheese with figs, almonds and homemade farmer's bread is typical of the Canary Islands. This heavier goat's cheese is in its prime when accompanied with a glass of rioja.

1 Cut the heads off the figs.
2 Scatter the goat's cheese over the figs and sprinkle almonds over the top.
3 Grill in the oven at 220°C for 8-10 minutes.

Makes 12 servings ★ 12 fresh figs ★ 100g fresh goat's cheese ★ 50g almond flakes

Tortilla de patatas
Potato Omelette

The potato omelette is one of the most well-known tapas in all of Spain. In Madrid, the tortilla is still frequently fried with a small onion (tortilla a la Española); in Valencia, it's eaten with rice or with leftover paella; and in Granada, tortillas with brains or bull's testicles are very popular. The omelette is usually eaten at room temperature.

1 Heat the oil in a deep frying pan and add the potatoes. Fry them on low heat with the lid on the pan until they are cooked through. This will take approximately 20 minutes. Stir occasionally. The potato slices must be soft, but not brown. When the potatoes are done, take them out of the pan and leave them to drain in a colander.

2 Sprinkle salt over the potatoes.

3 Lightly beat the eggs, so that the egg whites are mixed with the yolks. Add a little bit of salt.

4 Mix the potatoes into the egg mixture.

5 Heat some new oil, just enough to cover the bottom of the frying pan, and then add the egg and potato mixture. It is advisable to use an anti-stick frying pan.

6 Fry the mixture at a low temperature for 2 minutes. Occasionally shake the pan to prevent the mixture from sticking to the pan.

7 With the help of the lid or a large plate, flip the omelette. Place the plate or lid on top of the pan, hold it firmly and then turn the pan over. After that let the omelette slide from the plate or the lid into the frying pan and fry the other side for another 1 or 2 minutes.

olive oil ★ Salt ★ 6 eggs

Makes 8 servings ★ 750g potatoes, peeled and cut in thin slices ★ 350ml

Tortilla de espinacas

Spinach omelette

1 Fry the garlic in a large frying pan with some olive oil.
2 Add the spinach little by little. Allow the spinach to wilt and fry for another couple of minutes.
3 Leave the spinach cool down in a colander, squeeze out as much moisture as possible and chop the leaves.
4 Beat the eggs with cream, salt and pepper.
5 Stir the spinach into the egg mixture. Add the roasted pine nuts.
6 Fry the egg mixture in a frying pan, over a gentle heat, without stirring.
7 Turn the omelette over as it starts to set. With the help of the lid or a large plate, flip the omelette. Place the plate or lid on top of the pan, hold it firmly and then turn the pan over. After that, let the omelette slide from the plate or the lid into the frying pan and fry the other side. The omelette should still be relatively soft on the inside.

Tip: You can replace the pine nuts with 50g of chopped prawns.

Espinacas con pasas y piñones

Spinach with raisins and pine nuts

Makes 12 servings ★ 600 g raw spinach picked and washed. ★ 50ml olive oil ★ 50g pine nuts ★ 80g smoked ham, blanched (dipped in boiling water) and cut into small cubes ★ 50g raisins, soaked in warm water ★ 250ml water ★ Salt and freshly ground pepper

1 Heat the oil in a pan and cook the pine nuts until they are brown. Take them out of the pan and put them aside.

2 Cook the ham cubes in the same oil. Stir well.

3 Leave the raisins to drain and then cook them with the ham. After that, add them to the pine nuts.

4 At the highest heat, cook the raw spinach little by little. The spinach must be well drained.

5 Keep turning so that the released moisture evapo rates.

6 Add the ham, pine nuts and raisins once the spin ach has wilted.

7 Add salt and freshly ground pepper. Serve immediately.

Aros de cebolla

Deep-fried onion rings

1 Mix the egg yolk, oil, beer and flour together in a bowl. Season with salt and pepper.
2 In a separate bowl, beat the egg whites until they are firm.
3 Fold the egg mix into the batter.
4 Ensure that the onion rings are well covered in batter and then fry them in a deep frying pan until they are golden brown.
5 Leave them to drain on kitchen paper.
6 Put the onion rings in a dish and garnish them with some chives. Serve with alioli as a dipping sauce (see pan con alioli).

Tip: the spring onions also go well served with alioli (see recipe on page 31) or romesco sauce (see gambas con salsa romesco on page 85).

rings (don't use the small rings) ★ 2 eggs with egg yolks and white separated ★ 2 tablespoons of olive

and pepper ★ Fresh chives, chopped

oil ★ 200ml beer (lager) ★ 160g flour ★ Salt

According to the traditional Catalonian method of preparation, the calçots (Catalonian for 'spring onions') are roasted over a fire until they carbonize. The calçots are still extremely popular, which is to be seen during annual calçotadas; festivities based around the preparation rituals of the spring onion.

of red wine vinegar ★ 125ml olive oil ★ Pepper and salt

Calçots a la parilla

Roasted spring onions

1 Mix the peppers and garlic with the finely crushed almonds.
2 Then add the tomato, parsley and vinegar. Blend finely in a food processor or blender.
3 Add oil; Season with pepper and salt.
4 Grill the spring onions over an open fire or in a hot pan until they blacken.
5 Wrap the spring onions into aluminium foil and leave them for approximately 15 minutes.
6 Remove the outer layer of the onion and eat by dipping the soft interior into the sauce.

tomatoes, skinned, deseeded and cut into cubes ★ 1 tablespoon of parsley, chopped ★ 1 tablespoon

pers, with seeds removed ★ 6 cloves of garlic, chopped ★ 2

2 ★

Makes 2 servings ★ 2 potatoes, in cubes ★ Olive oil ★ 1 small onion, chopped ★ 1 clove of garlic, chopped ★ 200 g tomatoes, in small cubes ★ 1 tablespoon of tomato purée ★ Parsley, chopped ★ ¼ teaspoon of chilli pepper ★ A dash of tabasco ★ 1 laurel leaf ★ Sugar ★ Salt and pepper

Patatas bravas con salsa de tomate

Potatoes with tomato sauce

This very well-known tapa comes from Catalonia. The tomato sauce is sometimes mixed with alioli.

1 Fry the onion and garlic in olive oil until they become clear.
2 Add the tomatoes and leave to simmer.
3 Add the tomato purée, parsley, chilli pepper, tabasco and laurel leaf. Season with some sugar, salt and pepper.
4 Add a dash of water to the sauce and leave the covered pan to simmer for 30 minutes.
5 Leave the sauce to cool down.
6 In the meantime, fry the potato cubes until they are golden brown in the deep fryer or in the frying pan with some salt and olive oil.
7 Serve the potatoes with tomato sauce.

Aceitunas con limón y tomillo

Olives with lemon and thyme

Mix all of the ingredients and leave to marinate for a minimum of 24 hours.

Tip: Cut the olives into little pieces, which allows the marinade to penetrate more deeply.

Olives are great as a small and healthy tidbit. In Spain, they vary from simple manzanillas (Spanish green olives) to olives stuffed with anchovies or peppers. A true delicacy is the Aceitunas a la Sevillana, a typical Andalusian speciality. The marinade con limón y tomillo on this page is very popular.

Makes 6 servings ★ 300 g green olives with stones ★ Grated peel of 1 lemon ★ Juice of 1 lemon ★ 100ml olive oil ★ 1 red pepper, deseeded and cut in strips ★ 1 tablespoon of thyme, chopped

Aceitunas a la Sevillana

Sevillian Olives

Mix all of the ingredients and leave to marinate for a minimum of 24 hours.

of rosemary ★ 1 teaspoon of thyme ★ ½ teaspoon of fennel seed ★ 3 laurel leaves ★ 4 cloves of garlic ★ 4 anchovy fillets

Makes 6 servings ★ 300 g green olives ★ 6 tablespoon of vinegar ★ 100ml olive oil ★ ½ teaspoon

Makes 4 servings ★ 200 g black olives ★ 1 tablespoon of grated orange peel ★ 1 tablespoon of grated lemon peel ★ 2 tablespoons of lemon juice ★ Ground black pepper

Aceitunas con naranja

Olives with orange

Mix all of the ingredients and leave to marinate for a minimum of 24 hours.

1 tablespoon of fennel leaves, chopped ★ 10 coriander seeds ★ 1 clove of garlic, pressed ★ 4 tablespoons of olive oil ★ 1 tablespoon of lemon juice ★ Pepper and salt ★ 50g fennel, finely chopped ★ 200 g green olives

Aceitunas con hinojo

Olives with fennel

Mix all of the ingredients and leave to marinate for a minimum of 24 hours.

1 shallot, chopped finely ★ 1 sprig of rosemary ★ 2 garlic cloves ★ 1 teaspoon of sea salt ★ Black pepper ★ Lemon juice ★ Olive oil

Makes 6 servings ★ 11kg green asparagus ★ 3 tablespoon of blanched almonds, coarsely chopped ★

Espárragos con almendras

Asparagus with almonds

1 Clean the upper two thirds of each asparagus shoot.
2 Grill the asparagus in olive oil in the oven at 200°C for 10-12 minutes.
3 Grill the nuts in oil until they are light brown; then immediately add the rosemary sprig; the shallot and one clove of garlic are to be added after that.
4 Once this is done (after a couple of seconds) remove from the heat and immediately add some oil. The nuts must be brown and rosemary needles crispy. Remove the sprig.
5 Serve the asparagus with rosemary oil and a couple of drops of lemon juice as well as pepper and salt.

Ensalada de otoño

Autumn Salad

1 Chop up the eggs.
2 Fry the aubergine in olive oil for 3-4 minutes.
3 Then add the shallot and fry for 1 minute. Then add the tomato. Leave the mixture to cool down.
4 Mix this in with the olives, eggs, parsley, lemon juice and capers.
5 Season with pepper and salt.

50g tomatoes cut into cubes ★ 1 tablespoon of capers ★ 1 tablespoon

1 tablespoon of lemon juice ★ Pepper and salt

of flat leaf parsley, cut ★ 2 tablespoons of chopped black olives ★ 4 - 5 tablespoons of olive oil

Champiñones salteados

Baked mushrooms

Makes 4 servings ★ 2 tablespoon

Mushrooms prepared like this are not only delicious but they are ready and on the table within five minutes. Instead of ordinary white mushrooms, you also use cep or other fungi. To make this tapa extra special, add a dash of dry sherry.

1 Heat oil and add mushrooms.
2 Fry them over a high heat for 3-4 minutes.
3 Sprinkle with salt, pepper, garlic and parsley.
4 Serve immediately.

of olive oil ★ 250g small mushrooms ★ 1 clove of garlic, chopped ★ 1 tablespoon of parsley, chopped ★ Salt and pepper

Tapas de mariscos

Tapas with shellfish

chilli pepper or ½ teaspoon of cayenne pepper ★ 1 red pepper, roasted and cut

Gambas con salsa romesco

Prawns with romesco sauce

1 For the sauce put the almonds, garlic and pepper in a food processor. Blend the mixture in short blasts until it resembles fine breadcrumbs.
2 Add the roasted pepper and tomato, blending for a short while until all the ingredients are mixed together.
3 Pour the vinegar in and blend into a purée. While the food processor is on, allow the olive oil to gradually drizzle into the mix in a thin trickle, until a homogeneous consistency is achieved. The dressing will resemble a thickened cream. If necessary, add some water.
4 Season with salt and pepper and pour into a dish.
5 Cook the prawns until they are done and leave them to cool down.
6 Serve the prawns with the sauce at room temperature.

★ 1 Tomato ★ removed seeds and skin with pieces small into

125ml red wine vinegar ★ 250ml olive oil ★ Salt and pepper

★ 1 clove of garlic, finely chopped ★ Olive oil ★ 1 cup of prawns, peeled ★ For 1 portion

★ 1 Chilli pepper, in thin slices ★ Sea or table salt

Gambas al ajillo

Prawns with garlic

1 Heat the olive oil in a heat proof bowl.
2 Add the garlic and the pepper. Let them simmer for a while then add the prawns.
3 Add salt to taste.
4 Serve on French bread.

The traditional salsa romesco is always made with a base of roasted almonds and tastes delicious as a dip for fish and shellfish or also quite simply as a spread on toast. Originally from Catalonia, this sauce has been named after the hot peppers that grow in this region.

100ml olive

Makes 4 servings ★ 4 scallops in their shells, clean the shellfish and keep the shells ★

lemon juice ★ 1 teaspoon of sea salt ★ 1 tablespoon of parsley, chopped

Vieiras con pimientas
Scallops with peppers

1 Mix the oil, peppers, garlic, lemon juice, salt and olive oil.
2 Mix the shellfish with the oil mixture.
3 Divide the shellfish over their shells and grill or roast them in the shell.
4 Serve with toasted bread; garnish with parsley.

Tip: You can use mushrooms to fill the shells.
Marinate them in the same manner as the shellfish.

Mejillones a la vinagreta
Marinated mussels

Mussels are cooked as little as possible in Galicia, for example, steamed with just a little bit of salt and a laurel leaf, and then seasoned with an onion and wine marinade (a la vinagreta). With mejillones en escabeche, the marinade is poured over the mussels afterwards. This enhances the taste of the mussels and gives them a rich aroma. En escabeche is a time-honoured technique which conserves perishable products. In Asturia, sidra (cider) is traditionally drunk with this tapa.

1 Mix the oil, vinegar, capers, onion, pepper, parsley, salt and pepper in a dish. Put this mixture aside.
2 Clean the mussels well. Throw away any mussels that are not completely closed.
3 Put 250ml water in a frying pan with the slice of lemon and some salt and pepper.
4 Add the mussels and bring the water to the boil.
5 Take the mussels out of the water once they open. Leave them to cool down.
6 Take the mussels out of their shells and add them into the marinade. Put a lid on the dish and leave to stand overnight in the fridge.
7 Clean one half of each shell well and keep these also in the fridge.
8 Before serving, place the mussels back in their shell and spoon a little bit of marinade on top.

Mejillones en escabeche

Pickled mussels

1 Fry the mussels in olive oil, garlic and breadcrumbs.
2 Add the rest of the ingredients and leave to marinate for 24 hours.

Ensalada de pescado

French bread with fish salad

1 Cut the French loaf into pieces diagonally. Spread the pieces with the oil and place in a pre heated oven at 200°C (392F) for about 5 minutes, until they are brown and crispy.
2 Heat the fish stock and simmer the fish for 5 minutes.
3 Remove the skin and the bones from the fish and combine with the egg, potato and mayonnaise. Add salt and pepper to taste.
4 Spread the fish mixture onto the bread and garnish with parsley

Gambas a la plancha

Grilled Prawns

Makes 12 servings ★ 12 large prawns ★ 2 tablespoon of olive oil ★ 3 garlic cloves, chopped ★ Freshly ground pepper and sea salt ★ Some parsley, chopped ★ 1 lemon, in pieces

1 Grill the prawns either flat on a grill plate, or in a pan with olive oil.
2 Sprinkle with garlic as well as salt and pepper.
3 Garnish with parsley and serve with the lemon pieces.

All over Spain, prawns are preferably eaten a la plancha: cooked on a hot grill plate with some olive oil, parsley and sea salt. The advantage of this method of preparation is that it preserves their pure, refined flavour. If you do not have a grill plate, you can also cook the prawns on the barbecue. You can also try this recipe also with sardines!

For 4 servings ★ 4 tbsp olive oil ★ Juice of 1 lemon ★ 2 tbsp parsley, finely chopped ★ ½ onion, finely

Tostada de anchoa

Anchovy toast

1 Heat the oven to 200°C (392F).
2 Roast the bread until light brown.
3 Combine the oil with the parsley, lemon juice, onion, garlic and add salt and pepper to taste.
4 Spread each slice of bread with the oil mixture and finish off with 2 anchovy fillets.

Almejas con crema

Clams (Venus Shells) with cream

1 Fry the shallot and the garlic in oil until they are transparent.
2 Douse with wine, add the shells and cover the pan.
3 Bring to the boil, shake the shells once and boil again.
4 Take the shells out of the liquid, open them and remove the side of the shell without any flesh.
5 Reduce the liquid with cream into a sauce for 10-12 minutes.
6 On each shell put a little dollop of sauce.

Makes 6 servings ★ 500g clams (Venus Shells) ★ 2 tablespoons of olive oil ★ 2 shallots, chopped ★ 1 clove of garlic, chopped. ★ 100ml white wine ★ 200ml cream

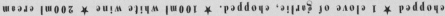

Makes 24 servings ★ 4 large Prawns, peeled ★100g breadcrumbs ★1 tablespoon of parsley, chopped ★ 1 teaspoon of salt ★Pepper ★3 tablespoons of flour ★ 150ml milk ★Oil for frying ★Wooden cocktail sticks

Gambas rebozadas

Breaded Prawns

1 Mix the breadcrumbs with parsley, salt and pepper.
2 Mix the flour and milk into a paste.
3 Thread the prawns onto a cocktail stick and put them in the flour paste and then into breadcrumbs.
4 Deep fry the prawns in oil until they are crispy.

Ostras con cava

Oysters in cava

Makes 12 servings ★ 12 raw oysters ★ 100ml oyster stock ★ 1 shallot, chopped ★ 50ml cream ★ 100ml cava (sparkling Spanish wine) ★ 50g hard butter, in cubes

1 Open the oysters and catch the liquid in a bowl.
2 Place the oysters in the deeper half of the shell.
3 Reduce the cava along with the oyster liquid, the shallot and cream down to half its volume.
4 Beat the cold cubes of butter through the sauce.
5 Cover the oysters with this liquid and place under the grill for 4-5 minutes until crispy.

Ensalada del mar

Seafood salad

1 Put the lemon juice and wine vinegar in a large bowl and stir in the olive oil slowly with a whisk.
2 Add the remaining ingredients and season with salt and pepper.
3 Add the chosen fish and leave to marinate for several hours before serving, preferably a day.

Tip: Softer fish types such as whiting and hake are better if first sprinkled with salt and left to rest for 30 minutes. This way, the flesh of the fish becomes slightly more firm and doesn't fall apart as quickly when left in the marinade. To poach the fish, you can use a fish stock or a mixture of water and white wine with some salt, a small onion, a carrot and some green herbs such as dill, thyme, parsley and celery.

Tapas con pescado

Tapas with fish

Calamares a la romana
Deep-fried squid

Deep-fried squid rings can be found in most tapas windows across Spain. They can be prepared using flour, even a little egg, but if you want an extra crispy covering, then a beer batter is what you really need.

1 Remove the tentacles and entrails from the squid.
2 Cut away the tentacles just above the eyes and remove the round bit of cartilage.
3 Under running water hold the purple coloured membrane of the tails.
4 Remove the cartilage from the tails, turn them inside out and rinse them out until they are clean.
5 Cut the squid into rings.
6 Leave them to drain and then dry them with a cloth.
7 Salt the squid rings and roll them in some flour. Shake the excess flour off before frying them.
8 Immerse the rings well in the hot oil and fry.
9 Serve warm, with lettuce and lemon wedges.

Makes 18 servings ★ 1kg squid ★ 100g flour ★ Salt ★ Olive oil for frying

Boquerones fritos
Deep fried anchovies

Makes 10 servings ★ 500g fresh anchovies ★ 100ml milk ★ 100g flour ★ Pepper and salt ★ Lemon quarters

1 Remove the entrails; and dry the fish.
2 Bathe them in milk and then dip them in the flour.
3 Deep fry them quickly until crispy, and then season with pepper and salt.
4 Serve with lemon wedges.

Fresh anchovies that have not been pickled is often eaten deep-fried in Spain. The fish are served in their entirety, along with head and bones. Boquerones taste delicious with a slice of lemon and a refreshing cerveza.

Salvia con anchoas

Sage with anchovy

1 Slice the anchovy fillets diagonally down the middle.
2 On each sage leaf place an equally sized anchovy fillet.
3 Thread the fillet and sage onto a cocktail stick.
4 Place them in milk and then afterwards put them in the flour.
5 Immerse the cocktail stick into the hot oil and deep fry until crispy.

parsley, cut ★ 2 laurel leaves, torn in bits ★ Salt and freshly ground pepper ★ 300ml olive oilv200ml vinegar

Makes 12 servings ★ 1kg sardines ★ 6 garlic cloves, chopped ★ Juice of one lemon ★ 1 tablespoon of

Sardinas al horno

Oven-cooked Sardines

1 Remove the entrails from the sardines and wash the fish clean.
2 Place a layer of fish in an ovenproof dish.
3 Spread garlic, lemon juice, parsley and laurel leaf on top and then sprinkle with salt and freshly ground pepper.
4 Place the rest of the fish on top and sprinkle this layer also with salt and pepper.
5 Then pour olive oil and vinegar over the fish. If the sardines aren't full covered, add some more oil and vinegar in the same ratio.
6 Put the dish in a moderately warm oven (170°C) for 30 minutes.
7 Leave the dish to cool in a cold place. If the dish is then left for a minimum of 24 hours to allow the flavours to combine, the taste will improve greatly.

Salmón con cava

Salmon in cava

2 tablespoons of lemon juice ★ 1 red onion, in rings ★ 1 tablespoon of capers ★ 4 sprigs of tarragon, just the leaves ★ Olive oil ★ Pepper and salt ★ 200ml cava ★ 8 salmon fillets, weighing 50g each ★ Makes 8 servings

1 Place the fillets in an oven dish.
2 Pour the cava, a dash of olive oil and the lemon juice on top.
3 Cover the fish with the onion rings, capers and tarragon. Sprinkle with pepper and salt.
4 Cover the dish and allow the dish to stew in an oven at 160°C for 10-14 minutes.

Salmón con cabrales

Salmon with cabrales

Asturia is the cheese region of Spain. In this area, no less than thirty cheeses are produced, of which the most well-known is undoubtedly cabrales. This blue cheese is made from raw cow, goat, and sheep milk. It is still matured traditionally in lime caves.

1 Roll the salmon fillets up and encase them in aluminium foil so that the flat upper and lower part stay uncovered.
2 Heat the baking tray and rub the tray as well as the salmon with oil.
3 Grill the fish for one minute on each side twice.
4 Sprinkle with cabrales and then place under the grill for 2-3 minutes. Now remove the aluminium foil.
5 Place the salmon on a plate and sprinkle with olive oil, pepper and salt.

Tip: serve with farmer's bread and a good glass of Asturian sidra (cider).

Makes 8 servings ★ 8 salmon fillets,

weighing 60g each ★ 150g cabrales (blue cheese), in pieces ★ Olive oil ★ Salt and pepper

crushed ★ Juice of 1 lemon ★ 10 black olives, stoned ★ Sprig of rosemary, cut into pieces ★ Sprig of thyme, cut into pieces

Ensalada de pulpo

Octopus (squid) salad

1 Bring the whole octopus (squid) to the boil with a pinch of salt and simmer for approx. 1 hour.
2 The octopus (squid) is cooked if you can prick the thickest part through with a small knife.
3 Plunge the half-peppers into a pan of boiling water. Remove immediately and rinse under cold water, remove the seeds and then dice.
4 Rinse the octopus (squid) under cold water and remove the blubbery substance between the arms. Cut the octopus (squid) into small pieces.
5 Add the peppers, onion, garlic, lemon juice, white wine, rosemary, thyme and olives.
6 Season with salt and pepper to taste and add lemon juice if you like. This mixture should have a sharp taste.

Tip: The flavour is even better if you marinade the pulpo overnight.

In Spain, 'octopus' (squid) isn't a generic name. Each kind of (squid) octopus has its own name. The large squid with tentacles is called 'calamares', best known when fried in rings. The small octopus (squid) that is cooked whole is called 'chiperones'. The really large octopus (squid) is called 'pulpo' and is often served in small pieces in a tapa.

1 clove garlic. ★ ½ yellow sweet peppers ★ ½ red and ★ 1 red onion, cut into rings ★ 1 white wine (1 oz)

For 4 servings ★ 1 small (squid) octopus, (approx 750g) (26.45oz) ★ 3 tbsp olive oil ★ ½ dsp (50ml/1.69

Bacalao al pilpil
Baked cod

The Basques particularly love to prepare their seafood al pilpil. Throughout this method of preparation, the contents of the pan are shaken continuously, which results in the gelatine from the skin of the fish, the fish bones or shells binding with the oil to form a jelly-like sauce.

1 Place the cod in cold water for a minimum of 24 hours. Refresh the water occasionally. Leave the fish to drain on a clean tea towel.
2 Fry the garlic and the pepper in olive oil until golden brown. Remove the mixture from the pan and set it aside.
3 In the same pan, fry the cod skin-side down for approximately 3 minutes (add some olive oil if necessary). Turn the fish and leave it to fry for another three minutes. Shake the pan continuously.
4 Turn the heat down, add some water and leave the fish to cook through for another 10-15 minutes. Shake the pan occasionally.
5 Fill little bowls with the fish and garnish with garlic and pepper.
6 Serve with baguette.

Tip: Try this recipe also with merluza (hake). Alternatively serve the fish with mojo verder (a green sauce from the Canary Islands). For this, you need a small amount of cumin, 4 cloves of garlic and a pinch salt. Mix it all in a food processor or blender. Add the leaves from a small bunch of coriander and slowly pour in 200ml olive oil. Leave this to blend until it becomes a sauce. Add fresh pepper and a dash of vinegar to taste.

Sepias fritas
Deep-fried squid

Makes 10 servings ★ 500g small squid (sepias or chipirones) ★

1 Thread the squid on to a cocktail stick
2 Mix 100ml milk with 4 tablespoons of flour into
  a paste.
3 Dip the threaded cocktail stick into the remaining
  flour and then into the paste.
4 Deep fry them quickly until they are brown and
  then season with pepper and salt.

Cocktail sticks ★ 100ml milk ★

100g flour ★ Pepper and salt ★ Lemon quarters

5 chicory heads ★ 100g anchovy fillets ★ 2 tablespoons of capers ★ 2 tablespoons of grated

or finely sliced mature cheese ★ 4-6

★ 5 witlofstronken ★

Makes 12 servings ★

tablespoons of olive oil ★ 1 garlic clove, chopped. ★ Black pepper

Endibias con anchoas

Chicory with anchovy

1 Peel the leaves from the chicory, and wash and dry them.
2 Spread the leaves over a plate and put an anchovy fillet
  on each leaf.
3 Along with the grated cheese, scatter the capers on top.
4 Season with olive oil, mixed with crushed garlic and
  some pepper.

Makes 4 servings ★ 1 red pepper, cut in 4 pieces, stalk and seeds removed ★ 8 anchovy

fillets ★ 3-4 tablespoons of olive oi

Pimientos con anchoas

Pepper with anchovy

The Northern Spanish cuisine, especially in Cantabria, is well-known for its anchovy specialities. The anchoas (pickled anchovy) are frequently served as tapa with olives, melon or pepper. Try this combination with chicory and capers and you'll change your mind about the perfect balance between salty and bitter.

1 Put two anchovy fillets on each piece of pepper
  and then wrap them in aluminium foil.
2 Place the pieces of pepper in an oven at 150°C
  for 40-45 minutes.
3 Serve with bread or pan tostada.

Tomate con atún

Tomato with tuna

1 Mix all the ingredients, with the exception of the twelve filling tomatoes.
2 Season with salt and pepper.
3 Stuff the tomatoes with the mixture.

half rings ★ 1 clove of garlic, chopped. ★ 4-6 tablespoons of olive oil ★ Pepper

Atún a la plancha

Grilled tuna

1 Grill the cubes of tuna in a hot pan or on a hot grill plate with olive oil.
2 Fry the onion and garlic.
3 Season with oil, salt and lemon juice.

Makes 10 servings ★ 500g tuna, in cubes ★ 1 red onion, cut into ★ 125g tin of tuna, chopped ★ 100ml olive oil ★ 4 dried tomatoes

and salt ★ 2 tablespoons of lemon juice

anchovy fillets from a tin, chopped ★

Makes 12 servings ★ 12 tomatoes (to stuff) ★ 100g black olives, chopped. ★ 1 tablespoon of capers★10

Banderillas
Spanish standards

Banderillas come from the north part of Spain and have been named after the coloured darts used by bullfighters. These tapas are made quickly and easily in advance. The ingredients can be varied in infinite combinations. Instead of anchovies, you can also try tuna or ham. Eggs, gherkins and prawns also work well with banderillas.

1 Thread all the ingredients onto a cocktail stick in the order given above.
2 Dip into a dressing of olive oil, parsley, garlic and vinegar (1 part vinegar to 3 parts oil).

Tip: prepare the banderillas in advance and preserve them. You can do this with vinegar, sugar, freshly ground pepper, salt, a laurel leaf and some thyme.

1 Make a large quantity of banderillas without anchovies and put them in an airtight glass jar.
2 Heat the vinegar with some sugar and herbs (pepper, salt, laurel, thyme) until the sugar has melted. Leave this to cool down.
3 Pour the vinegar mixture over the banderillas until they are covered.
4 Close the jar well. Leave to stand for a couple of days, so that the moisture is drawn into the banderillas.
5 This mixture will keep for several weeks. It is possible to add an anchovy just before serving.

Makes 10 servings ★ 500g fresh anchovy ★ 125ml white wine vinegar ★ Pepper and salt ★ 6 cloves of garlic, chopped. ★ 2 tablespoons of parsley, chopped. ★ 250ml olive oil

Boquerones en vinagre

Pickled anchovies

These fresh, sour anchovies are particularly refreshing, especially on warm summer days.

1 Cut open the belly of the fish and remove the back and head.
2 Clean the fish and dry them with paper.
3 Fold the fish open and sprinkle them with vinegar, pepper and salt.
4 Add enough water so that the fish are just covered.
5 Cover the dish and leave to marinate in the fridge overnight.
6 Take the fish out of the marinade and dry them.
7 Lay them in dishes and pour olive oil with garlic and parsley on top. Leave to stand for a short while so that the various flavours can combine.

Tapas con carne

Tapas with meat

1 lemon ★ 2 garlic cloves, chopped ★ 4 tablespoons of olive oil ★ Pepper and salt ★ Juice of ★ Dash of coriander powder ★ Dash of paprika powder ★ Dash of cumin ★ Dash of chilli powder ★ 8 wooden kebab sticks

Pinchos Morunos

Kebabs

1 Thread the cubes of meat onto the kebab stick which have first been soaked in water (this prevents them from burning).
2 Make a dressing with oregano, cumin, paprika powder, coriander and chilli powder, and add lemon juice, garlic and olive oil and pepper and salt.
3 Marinate the meat for least 1 hour in the fridge.
4 Grill or fry the kebabs until they are crispy and done.
5 Serve them lukewarm.

The various herbs in this popular tapa reveal a Moorish influence, although the Moors would have used lamb. Spaniards make these kebabs with pork as a preference.

Makes 8 servings ★ 400g pork, cut into cubes of lemxlcm ★ 1 teaspoon of oregano or thyme ★ Dash of chilli powder

Queso de cabra con jamón serrano

Goat's cheese with Serrano ham

Makes 12 servings ★ 12 pieces of soft goat's cheese, weighing 30g each ★ 12 slices of Serrano ham ★ 3 tablespoons of olive oil ★ 1 tablespoon of lemon juice ★ 1 clove of garlic, chopped

1 Wrap each piece of goat's cheese with a slice of Serrano ham.
2 Grill the parcels in a moderately hot frying pan for a short while.
3 Season with olive oil, lemon juice and garlic. Serve with baguettes or tostada.

Lomo con pasta de aceitunas

Beef steak with olive tapenade

1 In a blender or food processor, blend all the
  ingredients for the olive tapenade.
2 The tapenade can be made well in advance,
  and stays good for 4-6 days so long as it is
  kept chilled.
3 Cover the pieces of beef with the tapenade, roll
  them up and then skewer with a cocktail stick.
4 Fry the rolls on all sides until they are nicely
  browned and then season with pepper and salt.

150ml cava ★ 50ml olive oil ★ Pepper and salt

150ml cava ★ 50ml olive oil ★ Pepper and salt · 2 garlic bulbs, halved · 500g chicken fillets, in cubes · Makes 10 servings

Pollo con cava

Chicken in cava

Pollo al ajillo is known all over Spain. The chicken with garlic is given a little something extra with a considerable shot of cava, the Spanish 'cellar variant' of French champagne, which makes this tapa even more enjoyable.

1 Place the chicken fillets in an oven dish.
2 Put the garlic in as well and then sprinkle the garlic with pepper and salt. Pour the cava and olive oil on top.
3 Cover the dish and put it in the oven at 160°C for 30 minutes.
4 Remove the lid and grill the pieces of chicken under the grill until crispy and brown.
5 Serve in dishes with garlic, which has sweetened in the meantime.

Patatas con tocino y chorizo

Roasted potato with bacon and chorizo

1 Fry the shallots with the garlic until they are transparent. Add the pepper, bacon and sausage.
2 Fry for another two minutes and then add the potatoes slices.

Tip: You can eat this tapa both warm and cold.

★ 150g smoked bacon, in cubes ★ ★ 150g chorizo, in cubes ★ Olive oil

Chorizo con sidra Chorizo in cider

1 Fry the onion and the garlic in olive oil until they are golden brown.
2 Add the chorizo.
3 Pour the cider on top and bring to the boil. Leave to simmer on a low heat for no more than 20 minutes until the cider has evaporated completely.
4 Serve the chorizo cubes in a dish garnished with some parsley.

Olive oil

Cordero con aceitunas

Lamb with olives

Makes 8 servings ★ 8 pieces of lamb, weighing 60g each ★ 3-4 tablespoons of olive oil ★ 2 tablespoons of breadcrumbs ★ 1 tablespoon of parsley, chopped ★ 2 garlic cloves, chopped ★ 2 tablespoons of olives, chopped ★ Pepper and salt

1 Fry the pieces of lamb in a hot pan with a little oil for 2-3 minutes until browned.
2 Add the rest of the ingredients and cook for another minute or two.

Migas del pastor

Shepherd's bread

Once upon a time, migas were the provisions of shepherds. These days, they are a delicacy that is often eaten on festive occasions. During their long journeys, shepherds crumbled their old bread (migas literally means breadcrumbs) and baked it with some garlic and paprika powder in lamb's fat. In Aragon, where the traditional migas del pastor comes from, the breadcrumbs are served with grapes and chorizo. Lovers of the sweet variant soak the bread first in milk and then fry it in sugar and cinnamon.

1 Cut the bread in cubes the day beforehand and leave out to dry.
2 Heat the oil and fry the bacon, sausage and garlic for approximately 4 minutes. Then add the bread and fry for 4 minutes.
3 Sprinkle with salt.

Makes 8 servings ★ 250 g old bread ★ 80ml olive oil ★ 150g smoked bacon, in cubes ★ 150g chorizo, in bits ★ 4 garlic cloves, chopped

Albóndigas con salsa de tomate

Meatballs in tomato sauce

This traditional tapa is generally made from veal or pork. In Andalusia, the albóndigas are not only popular in dining establishments but also form a very important part of home cooking. Generally the meatballs are served in a tomato sauce but sometimes they are also served with a cognac or almond sauce.

1 First make the sauce. Fry the onion and the carrot on a low fire in olive oil for 10 minutes.
2 Add the flour and continue to stir well until the mixture browns.
3 Then add the tomato purée and fry for a minute. Continue to stir.
4 Dampen the mixture with the white wine.
5 Then add the stock, season with salt and leave the sauce to cook for another 20 minutes.
6 In the meantime, make the meatballs. Soak the bread in milk and squeeze out the liquid. Mix it in with the meat, parsley and garlic. Season the mixture with salt and then add the eggs. Mix well.
7 Roll the mixture into little balls and then flour them.
8 Fry a couple of meatballs at a time in a frying pan with olive oil until they are browned. Then put them into an ovenproof dish.
9 Blend the sauce in the food processor. Pour the sauce over the meatballs and leave to cook in the oven at 180°C for 25 minutes.

Riñones al jerez

Veal kidneys with sherry

Sherry is not only the best companion to tapas but also is the preferred drink in the kitchen. Its name, Jerez, originates from the region surrounding Jerez de la Frontera. In Spain sherry is drunk as a white wine. The drink is divided into varying degrees of sweetness. Fino (lightly salty with a zest of almond) and manzanilla (strong, slightly spicy taste) are dry. Amontillado (nutty taste) is medium sweet; oloroso (ripe sherry, reminiscent of white port) is sweet.

1 Heat the oil, dust the kidneys in flour and put them in the hot oil.
2 Add the garlic and shallot, and fry until light brown
3 Add the sherry, salt and pepper.
4 Leave to simmer for 16-20 minutes until the kidneys are done.
5 Serve the kidneys with bread and sprinkle with parsley.

parsley, chopped ★ 1 tablespoon of ★ Salt and pepper ★ 100ml dry sherry ★ 1 shallot, shredded ★ 2 garlic cloves, chopped ★ oil

Makes 6 servings ★ 250 g veal kidneys, chopped into pieces ★ 1 tablespoon of flour ★ 3 tablespoons of olive

Salpicón de pollo
Chicken salad

1 Fry the chicken fillets in olive oil for 5 minutes until done. Leave them to cool down.
2 Mix the onion, garlic, vinegar, capers, avocado, tomatoes, radishes and olives in a dish.
3 Add the potatoes and chicken fillets and stir everything together well. Stir in the mayonnaise and salt and pepper according to taste. Serve at room temperature.

Pollo a la cerveza

Chicken with beer

1 Fry the chicken in olive oil until light brown in a casserole dish.
2 Sauté the onion and garlic for one minute.
3 Leave the chicken in a pot covered with lid.
4 Pour the beer into the casserole. Continue to stir while removing the baked leftovers.
5 Pour this mixture over the chicken.
6 Add brown sugar, vinegar, herbs, salt and pepper.
7 Leave everything to stew for approximately 25-35 minutes until the chicken is done.

Tip: This is lovely both warm and cold! Instead of drumsticks, you could also use wings.

Patatas con jamón serrano

Potatoes with Serrano ham

1 Heat a heavy frying pan.
2 Cut the potatoes into very small matchsticks.
3 Mix the slivers with pepper and salt, Serrano ham and garlic.
4 Fry little cakes of the potato matchsticks in a little hot oil.

1 clove of garlic, chopped ★ 2-4 tablespoons of olive oil ★ Pepper and salt

For 16 balls ★ 250g (8.81 oz) minced beef (ground beef) ★ 1 egg, lightly beaten ★ 100g (3.52 oz) chorizo, finely chopped ★ 1 tbsp olive oil ★ 1 tbsp tomato puree ★ 1 bunch parsley, finely chopped ★ 10 black olives, finely chopped ★ Salt and pepper

Albóndigas con chorizo
Chorizo balls

1 Combine the minced (ground) beef with the egg, chorizo and tomato puree and add salt and pepper to taste.
2 Bind the mixture with breadcrumbs if necessary. Form the mixture into small round balls.
3 Fry the balls in the oil until they turn golden brown, then add the olives. Simmer for 5 minutes.
4 Garnish with parsley.

finely chopped ★ 3 garlic cloves, crushed ★ 100g tinned

Makes 4 servings ★ 200 g Serrano ham, in cubes ★ Olive oil ★ 1 onion

broad beans ★ 1 tablespoon of parsley, chopped ★ Pepper and salt

Habas con jamón

Broad beans with ham

1 Fry the onion and garlic in some olive oil.
2 Add the ham and fry for another minute or two.
3 Then add the broad beans and fry them together.
4 Season with pepper and salt. Garnish with parsley.

Caldereta de cordero

Lamb stew

Makes 20 servings ★ 1 kgshoulder of lamb, without the bone and cut into cubes ★ 1 green Spanish pepper, made from fresh white bread ★ 2 teaspoons of mild paprika powder ★ A pinch of cumin powder

1 Put the meat into a casserole dish and pour in enough cold water so that the meat is covered.
2 Boil and then remove the foam. Then add the green pepper, tomatoes, onion, clove, parsley, laurel and the head of garlic, as well as a dash of oil and some salt. Leave the meat to simmer for 1.5-2 hours, until it is soft.
3 Crush the pepper grains in a mortar, add the bread crumbs, paprika powder and cumin and mix into a paste.
4 Mix this into the liquid and leave to simmer for another couple of minutes.
5 Serve in small dishes.

(left margin) **Olive oil ★ Salt ★ 5 pepper corns ★ 1 large tablespoon of breadcrumbs**

(right margin) **deseeded and cut into pieces ★ 2 to ...s, skinned and cut into pieces ★ 1 onion,**

(bottom margin) **coarsely chopped ★ 1 clove ★ Handful of flat leaf parsley, chopped. ★ 1 laurel leaf ★ 1 head of garlic ★**

Paquetes y buñuelos

Fritters and wraps

Makes 4 servings ★ 100 g rozen spinach, defrosted ★ Dill ★ Pepper and salt ★ 4 sheets of filo pastry ★ 1 egg, beaten ★ 1 onion, chopped ★ 1 tomato, chopped ★ 1 leek leaf, cut into strands

Paquetes de espinacas

Spinach wraps

1 Season the spinach with pepper, salt and dill.
2 Brush the filo pastry with some egg.
3 Put the spinach, some onion and tomato on top.
4 Fold the pastry around the spinach and close it with a strand of leek. Deep fry the wraps until brown and crispy.

There are two types of buñuelos: deep fried pastry wraps or balls. The filling varies from ham, chorizo or cheese to various types of vegetable and bacalao (cod).

Makes 8 servings ★ 2 egg whites ★ 1 cup of grated Manchego (cheese) ★ Cayenne pepper ★ 3 teaspoon of flour ★ 8 small cubes of Serrano ham ★ Oil for deep frying

Buñuelos de jamón y queso

Ham and cheese wraps

1 Beat the egg whites into peaks.
2 Stir in the cheese, cayenne pepper and flour.
3 With two spoons, make eight balls from the mixture and push the ham cubes into the middle.
4 Deep fry the balls until golden brown.

Buñuelos de bacalao

Cod Balls

1 Clean the cod well.
2 Blend the fish with the bread in
   the blender; then add the egg,
   garlic, olive oil, milk and pepper.
3 With two spoons, make balls from
   the mixture.
4 Deep-fat fry the balls in olive oil
   until golden brown.

Empanadillas
Pastry wraps (basic recipe)

These days you can't imagine empanadas and empanadillas (small empenadas for one person) as not being part of Spanish cuisine. They are often seen on the menu in Spanish tapas bars. However, these wraps, filled with vegetables, meat or fish, were once only to be found in Galicia. They were commonly eaten by pilgrims on their way to Santiago de Compostella.

1 Heat the water in a pan with salt, oil and the butter, until the butter has melted.
2 Transfer the mixture into a mixing bowl and add the flour. Stir until all the liquid has been absorbed
3 Add the egg and stir it in well.
4 Dust the work surface with flour and put the pastry on top.
5 Knead the pastry until it is soft and elastic and does not stick to the surface any more.
6 Put the pastry back in the bowl, cover and leave to stand for 45 minutes.
7 Roll the pastry into a thin sheet.
8 Cut circles of approximately 10cm in diameter.

Makes 20 empanadillas

★ 125 ml water ★ ½ teaspoon of salt ★ 25ml oil ★ 25 tablespoon of butter ★ 250g flour ★ 1 small egg

Makes 20 empanadillas ★ 1 tablespoon of olive oil ★ 1 onion, chopped ★ 2 tins of tuna (weighing approximately 225g each) ★ 75ml tomato sauce ★ 1 roasted pepper, see recipe pimientos), chopped ★ 2 tomatoes, peeled and chopped ★ 1 tablespoon of parsley, chopped ★ 1 hardboiled egg, finely chopped ★ Salt and freshly ground pepper ★ 20 cut-outs of pastry wraps for empanadillas (see previous recipe) ★ Possibly 2 eggs

Empanadillas de atún

Pastry wraps with tuna

1 Heat the olive oil in a frying pan. Fry the onion until it is transparent.
2 Leave the tuna to drain and mash it finely.
3 Add the tuna in with the tomato sauce, pimientos, tomato and parsley to the mixture in the pan.
4 Add some salt and pepper.
5 Leave for approximately 10 minutes to simmer until it thickens.
6 Take the pan from the heat and scatter the hardboiled egg over the mixture.
7 Place a good tablespoon of filling in the middle of each pastry wrap. Fold the cut-out rounds shut and use a fork to press the edges together.
8 You can cook the empanadillas in several ways:
   • in a high-sided frying pan, with a large quantity of olive oil;
   • in a deep fryer;
   • in a hot oven (175°C) for 25 minutes. If you do cook them in the oven, first beat two eggs with a little bit of water in a sepa rate bowl and then brush the mixture over the empanadillas before you put them in the oven.

olive oil ★ 1 onion, chopped ★ 1 clove of garlic, crushed ★ Salt and pepper ★ 2 tablespoons of raisins, soaked in warm water ★ 1 tablespoon of parsley, chopped ★ 1 teaspoon of oregano ★ A dash of paprika powder ★ 1 teaspoon of ground cumin ★ 2 tablespoons of dry white wine ★ 2 teaspoons of tomato sauce ★ 1 hardboiled egg, finely mashed ★ 20 cut-outs of pastry wraps for empanadillas: see previous recipe ★ 2 eggs (optional: depends on the method of cooking) ★ 2 tablespoons of 100g beef, minced ★ 100g pork, minced ★ 100 g veal, minced ★ Makes 20 empanadillas

empanadillas: see previous recipe ★ 2 eggs (optional: depends on the method of cooking)

Empanadillas de carne

Pastry wraps with meat

1 Heat the oil in a frying pan and fry the onion with the garlic until transparent.
2 Add the veal, pork and beef and fry on a moderate heat until the meat browns.
3 Season well with salt and pepper.
4 Leave the raisins to drain and add them along with the parsley, oregano, paprika powder, cumin, wine, tomato sauce and hardboiled egg to the meat mixture. Put the lid on the pan and leave the mixture to simmer for approximately five minutes.
5 In the middle of each pastry wrap, put a good tablespoon of filling.
6 Fold the cut-out rounds shut and using a fork press the edges together.
7 You can cook the empanadillas in several manners:
   • in a high-sided frying pan, with a large quantity of olive oil;
   • in a deep fryer;
   • in a hot oven (175°C) for 25 minutes. If you do cook them in the oven, first beat two eggs with a little bit of water in a separate bowl and then brush the mixture over the empanadillas before you put them in the oven.

Index